Genre Nonfiction

 Essential Question
How do animals survive in nature?

Go, Gator!

by Diane Furuichi

CHAPTER 1
Where Alligators Live

What is that over there? It looks like a bumpy log, but it's not. It's an alligator in a warm **swamp**. The swamp is somewhere on the southeast coast of the United States.

The map shows where alligators live. A lot of alligators live in Florida.

Alligators live in many states, from North Carolina to Texas.

United States

Atlantic Ocean

Gulf of Mexico

This alligator floats just below the surface of the water. Only its eyes and nose stick out so the alligator can see and breathe. The rest of the body hides safely under the water.

An alligator's skin blends in with the swamp. The skin is very tough because it's covered with spikes. Inside each spike is a bone.

The skin acts like armor. It protects the alligator from the bites of **venomous** snakes and other animals.

CHAPTER 2
What Alligators Eat

Alligators are **carnivores,** or meat eaters. They search for food at night. They have about 75 very sharp teeth. Their jaws can crush bones and shells.

Alligators seek food when they are hungry. When they sense something moving in the dark—*SNAP!*

What did the hunter catch tonight? It might be a small animal, such as a snake. It could be a turtle or a raccoon.

Or it might be much larger, like a deer. If the **prey** was small, the meal was swallowed whole.

Alligators eat small animals such as raccoons like this.

Alligators lie in the sun to stay warm.

If its meal was large, the alligator won't have to eat again for a very long time.

One filling meal can be enough for more than a year.

Alligators move quickly on land. Their legs are short but strong. Look at the feet. The front feet have five toes, but the back feet have only four.

Alligators swim quickly, too. Their long, flat tail is very strong. To swim, alligators whip their tail back and forth through the water.

Alligators can run fast if they have to.

back foot

CHAPTER 3
Alligators and Their Young

Baby alligators hatch from eggs. The mom makes a nest on land and lays her eggs in the nest. She doesn't sit on the eggs. This mom is just too big. She would crush them! But she stays close to keep the eggs safe until they hatch.

George Shelley/Corbis

The mom takes cares of her babies for two or three years. After that, the babies go off on their own. They can start to find their own food. They are ready to take good care of themselves.

Baby alligators have yellow stripes.

Respond to

Reading

Retell

Use your own words
to retell important
details in *Go, Gator!*

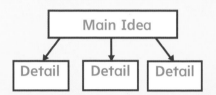

Text Evidence

1. Look at page 8. What is unusual
   about an alligator's feet? Main Idea
   and Key Details

2. Look at pages 9 and 10. What is
   the main idea of this chapter? Main
   Idea and Key Details

3. Is *Go, Gator!* a work of fiction or
   nonfiction? How do you know? Genre

Compare Texts

Alligators are tough, fierce hunters. Read a poem about animals that are small and gentle.

Ducklings

Fuzzy little quacking puffs
All dressed up in yellow fluff.

Waddling as they cross
   a street
Paddling with their big
   webbed feet
Swimming down the stream
   to play
Downy ducklings on
   their way.

Mama duck will teach
 her brood
How to dive to find
 their food.
Mama duck will lead
 her pack
All the way downstream
 and back!
This busy day has been
 the best.
Now the ducklings have
 to rest!

Make Connections

How are the ducklings similar to the baby alligators in *Go, Gator!*

Text to Text

Glossary

carnivores *(KAHRN-i-vorz)* animals that eat the flesh of other animals *(page 5)*

prey *(PRAY)* animals hunted by other animals for food *(page 6)*

swamp *(SWOMP)* watery land *(page 2)*

venomous *(VEN-uhm-us)* having a poisonous bite *(page 4)*

Index

Focus on Science

Purpose To observe wild animals that live near you

What to Do

Step 1 ▶ Look for animals that live outdoors in your neighborhood.

Step 2 ▶ Make a chart like the one below. Write the names of animals you see.

What I Saw	Where I Saw It	What It Was Doing

Step 3 ▶ Write a short nonfiction story about one of the animals in your chart. Draw pictures to go with your nonfiction story.

Conclusion Share what you learned.